Sue A. Hershkowitz, CSP

POWER
SALES
WRITING

**What Every
Sales Person
Needs to
Know to Turn
Prospects
Into Buyers**

Power Sales Writing:
What Every Sales Person Needs
To Know To Turn Prospects Into Clients!

Sue A. Hershkowitz

Printed in the United States of America.
Cover by Ad Graphics. 800/386-6196
Library of Congress: 95 - 80030
ISBN: 0-9648464-0-3

Published by:
High Impact Publications
a subsidiary of High Impact Presentations
Scottsdale, AZ 85254

To order more copies of this book, or to receive a complete catalog of Sue's products, including information on her professional speaking and consultation services, please call:

V. 1-602-996-8864
F. 1-602-996-6667
E-Mail
AOL: Hershk
Compuserve: 74117,56

ACKNOWLEDGMENTS

This book is a direct result of the thousands and thousands of Power Writing workshop attendees, who have asked for more - more training, more ideas, more "stuff" for them to refer to after the glow of the workshop has dimmed. Thank you for motivating me to finally put these advanced sales writing techniques in writing!

Thank you to Larry Winget, my colleague in the National Speakers Association, who inspired me to have my dream and to my friend, Joe Charbonneau, CSP, CPAE, who taught me where to begin. Thank you to Evangeline Ismael for helping with the final touches. Sometimes it's difficult to see the trees for the forest, and I appreciate your guidance. Thank you to my family for understanding my passion with this book and my many hours at the computer. Most of all, thank you to my coordinator, office administrator and keeper of my sanity, Paula Wigboldy, for her constant inspiration and support.

Dedicated to my parents
Lois and Phil Hershkowitz
who taught me the meaning of the word
mensch
and to my son
Michael
who is fast becoming one

TABLE OF CONTENTS

INTRODUCTION

"As soon as you move one step up from the bottom, your effectiveness depends on your ability to reach others through the written or spoken word."
— Peter Drucker

"Perhaps the one most vital skill today is the ability to write well..."
— Wall Street Journal

"There is no such thing as 'soft sell' and 'hard sell.' There is only 'smart sell' and 'stupid sell'!"
— Charles Brower

"The ability to write is fast becoming a survival skill in today's marketplace," according to <u>Sales & Marketing Management</u> magazine. Even if you're only a survivor, you'll need this book. If you're a winner, a champion, a sales professional who isn't willing to settle for anything but the best, *these ideas will dramatically increase the amount of money you put in your own pocket* and the profitability of the organization you represent!

Our fast–paced lives have limited our time and shortened our attention span. You have five seconds to grab the reader's attention in the direct mail you send out. You have just a few more seconds to get your reader's attention for anything else you write.

You need to write effective letters...and you need to learn it now. You've come to the right place.

You won't find any theory or esoteric stuff in these pages, so if that's what you're looking for, please do us both a favor and put the book down. Instead, the book is filled with:

- simple-to-use techniques that give you the confidence you need to write powerfully and professionally

- tips to use your selling time more effectively and profitably

- quick, specific examples of how you can implement the strategies to gain that competitive edge

- practical tips to help your letters and proposals stand out from the crowd

- down-to-earth, field–tested ideas to build greater rapport and cement relationships with prospects, clients, customers

Use just one of the ideas within and you'll pay for the book many times over. Implement more than one idea and the sky is the limit! ⑤

PART I

GETTING STARTED WITHOUT PROCRASTINATION OR PANIC

Writing <u>is</u> as easy as talking—honest! Here are the tips you need to face that blank paper or computer screen with a confidence you may never have had before.

The first part of this book will do more than get you started—You'll gain easy to use techniques to help you— yes, you!—use your sales letters as a tool for creating more sales. Go on...read!

IF YOU CAN TALK, YOU CAN WRITE

"Just do it!"
— Nike commercial

"The illiterate of the future are not those who cannot read and write; the illiterate of the future are those who cannot learn, unlearn and relearn."
— Alvin Toffler

Unbelievable. That prospect that you've been trying to get to accept your call, turns out to be your racquetball partner. You play a great game and as you walk together to the locker room you hear those magic words, "Aren't you the one who keeps calling me about (fill in your product/service/solution). So tell me what you have to offer."

What a gift! You start talking. You yip and yap, and use your opportunity to explain how you have the finest, best, most cost effective, greatest value widget of all time...you go for it.

Well, guess what? Writing is yipping and yapping, too. It's less embarrassing than talking (you know, the open mouth, insert foot syndrome?) and it's more thorough because unlike the time you made a sales presentation and forgot the most important benefit you had to offer, you'll have time to review and rewrite.

Best of all, writing is as easy as talking...once you discover a series of little known tactics and strategies that you have before you.

Picture this. The phone rings in your office. Your sales manager wants to know if you're still interested in winning that trip to the Caymans. Of course you are and you tell her so and you tell her why you are and what you'll do to make it happen. Then she asks you to put all that in writing.

Panic sets in. You'd rather put bamboo shoots under your nails than write...The Memo. You stare at the computer screen. You get another cup of coffee. You check out the weather.

Not anymore! That's how you used to operate. Now, you'll simply start talking on the page. There is always time to fix (edit) later. All you want to do is get your words on the page at this point. Talk out what you would say if you only had five minutes in the elevator with her.

See how easy this is! ❺

Your "Magic" Plan: Know Why You're Writing

"Without a plan, it doesn't matter which way you're going."

— Lewis Carroll

"I never worry about where the puck is. I never worry about where the puck was. I only focus on where the puck is going."

— Wayne Gretsky

If you lived in Lake Tahoe, would you simply get into your car, without a map, compass or AAA Triptik and drive to Bangor, Maine? If you did, you'd most likely wind up getting lost a few times or going out of your way.

The detour might be fun for you. Interesting new sights. An adventure. Something else to think about.

Your readers won't be quite so adventurous. Take them on a detour and you'll lose 'em.

Does the reader actually read?

A major US bank conducted research with 400 executives across the USA. Each executive received a hard copy of a three page memo. About two–thirds down the second page, the researchers had placed this message:

> "This memo is part of a research project. If you've read this far, please punch in a twelve-digit code to indicate you've read it. To thank you for your time, we will send you a one hundred dollar gift certificate."

Okay. So you're much richer than I am and it's beneath you to punch in the twelve–digit code. Or it's too much of an effort. Or you just don't feel like it and the incentive isn't enough.

Some people must feel that way because out of the 400 executives receiving the memo, only 17 punched in that code. (We think one person read it and told sixteen buddies!)

Mapping out your thoughts

By planning what you're going to "say;" by taking the time (about two minutes) to answer a few questions <u>before</u> you talk it out on the page or computer screen, you can save up to 80% of the time you spend writing. (Did you read that—up to 80%!) That's selling time. That's money in the bank. That pays for this book and last night's dinner and the new Ferrari. Well, almost!

The magic? **Know why you're writing.** ⑤

GETTING RESULTS MEANS KNOWING WHAT RESULT YOU WANT

*"Businesses' failure to communicate is awesome.
Two–thirds of all customer dissatisfaction is directly
related to businesses' failure to communicate."*
— Richard Whitely; The Forum Corporation

*"First comes thought, then organization of that
thought into ideas and plans; then transformation
of those plans into reality. The beginning...is in your
imagination."*
— Napoleon Hill

"Begin with the end in mind."
— Stephen Covey

When Stephen Covey said, "Begin with the end in mind," he meant it on a philosophical level. Understand where you're going. Develop goals. Know what you want from every venture, every day, every relationship.

Covey's words apply equally to writing. From now on, before you begin any—every—document, start by asking some very easy and vital questions:

<u>Why am I writing?</u>
<u>What do I want to say?</u>
<u>What must I accomplish?</u>

Easy questions, right? Simple? You bet. Pretty basic? Absolutely.

They're basic and they work...every time

I was presenting a two day writing program for a large and taxing (ha, ha!) government agency. When they accepted my bid, they sent me an agreement that said they could change, modify or delete anything from the manual I submitted. I designed this manual, as I do in every corporate writing program I present, by reviewing the writing samples (approximately 500 in this case!) they sent to me. The three questions I listed above (and one more) were included in the workbook.

The coordinator called me and said, "No, no, no. Those four questions you have at the beginning of the manual are way too basic for us. All of my people have at least four–year degrees. We do a very specialized type of writing around here. These questions will never work."

I used every counseling strategy I had acquired from my degree program to counsel him. "Yes, you're right. They do look basic. And I have seen them work...I've seen them save people frustration. I've seen them cut writing time by more than half. I've watched people who never knew how to start writing—start quickly and efficiently. I'll be there two days...we can modify and delete then. May I be permitted to introduce them?"

"Okay, as long as you realize they'll never work around here," he said.

Today, three locations of this large, taxing organization have these questions programmed into their software. Every time anyone starts to write, the questions pop up first.

Don't believe it? Try it out

So here it comes—your first opportunity to use what you've learned. Someone once said if you give a man/woman a fish, he/she has dinner for a night. If you teach him/her to fish, he/she has dinner forever. (Lousy paraphrase, good analogy.)

Start fishing! Here it is:

You met with your prospect, Liz Libert, earlier today and because your computer was down you couldn't give her the information she needed immediately. By the time you get back to your hotel room/office, the system is up and working fine and praise be, you have exactly what she is looking for. (Fill this in for your product or service. You have the rates and dates, if you're a hotelier. You have the perfect house, if you're a professional real estate agent. You have the exact dates management needed, if you're a meeting planner...you get the picture.)

Your flight/first meeting tomorrow is at 6:00 AM and you want to have the fax/proposal/e-mail waiting for her when she arrives at work.

O.K., now write it. Yes...you! Take out your pen or turn on your computer and start writing.

How did you start? Did you plunge right in and begin "Dear Liz"? If you did, credit yourself with two points for talking it out on the page.

If you started by answering the three questions I gave you in this very section, score fifty big ones!

Why am I writing?

To tell Liz we have exactly what she wants

What do I want to say?

We can deliver it Thursday as long as I get her approval

What do I want to accomplish?

Close the sale

P.S. If you didn't write the letter this time, you're forgiven. Write it now. You bought this book to learn, right? You wanna make more money, right?   Reading isn't going to do it! Learning how to do it and doing it, will do it!

Helpful hint

P.P.S. Be careful about using a P.S. in a sales letter. It can indicate to your reader (buyer) that you're disorganized. "Oh, by the way, psst, P.S. I just thought of something else to tell you: The price of those things is....!"

An effective P.S. should not be a new idea. It is a rephrased benefit guaranteed to seduce your reader to go back to read the letter! Use your strongest what's-in-it-for-the-buyer benefit. Make it clear and focused. (More later!) 💲

CHAPTER

4

THE KEY: KNOW THE EXACT ACTION YOU WANT THE READER TO TAKE

"As soon as you move one step up from the bottom, your effectiveness depends on your ability to reach others through the written or spoken word."
— Peter Drucker

"What makes men great is their ability to decide what is important, and then focus their attention on it."
— Goethe

What makes both men and women great, and rich, is their ability to know exactly what they want from the prospect/client/customer before committing anything to paper.

The great and the rich (sales professional) can tell you exactly what the reader will do, or how the reader will react immediately after he or she finishes reading the message.

Here's the question:

What exact action or reaction do you want your reader to have, or to take, as soon as he or she finishes reading your letter?

Do you want him to do something when he is done with your sales proposal? Is he supposed to call you to let you know he wants to do business with you, or to take the time to explain that yes, he received your packet of information. Or maybe, that he never wants to hear from anyone again who would be foolish enough to expect him, the reader, to follow up instead of you, the salesperson, following up with him??? (More about this in a later section!)

Do you want her to say something? To whom? About what? Do you want her to take some sort of action? What? Should she read your proposal and throw it away? Should she file it? Why? Should she expect your call?

Get specific before you pick up the pen

Before you write, determine clearly, specifically and exactly what you want your reader to do when he or she finishes reading. And then (this is going to be profound!), tell them!

What action or reaction do I want as soon as Liz finishes reading?

I want her to sign my memo and fax it back with her authorization to go ahead.

See if this doesn't cover it:

Dear Liz,

Great news! We can deliver your order of 1,900 discs to your Long Island warehouse as early as noon, Thursday. The price is .05 per disc and the terms are net thirty days, as we discussed.

All I need to go ahead with this shipment is your authorization on this memo. Please initial next to your name and add your pass code. I'll take care of the rest of the details.

Liz, these discs are top quality and we stand behind every purchase with our 24-hour response line and one hundred percent satisfaction guarantee.

I'll fax you your confirmation for your records as soon as I receive your authorization.

Sincerely,

MAKE IT EASY FOR THE READER TO BUY FROM YOU

"To succeed, jump as quickly at opportunities as you do at conclusions."

— Benjamin Franklin

"You have removed most of the roadblocks to success when you have learned the difference between movement and direction."

— Joe L. Griffith

Are you paid to sell or tell? If you're like the other thousands of sales people I work with in the Power Sales Letter Writing sessions I present around the globe, you are definitely paid to sell. Yet, when you write, you tell.

This sound familiar?

If you have any questions, please do not hesitate to call.

I look forward to hearing from you soon.

I'll follow up with you soon. In the interim, if you have questions, please feel free to contact me.

I grow gray hair every time I read "forceful, dynamic sales closings" like the ones I just listed. (In case you skimmed that sentence, it was a joke. Those closings are neither forceful, dynamic nor even _sales_ closings!) So if I am really gray when we meet, you and your sales letter/proposal closings may be responsible!

Take control of your communication

Either tell the reader exactly what you want him or her to do, or tell the reader exactly what you will do. But tell the reader something! Your action step should be clear and specific.

Michael, I'll follow up with you September 9 to see how you would like to proceed.

Maria, I'll call you February 14 to see how we might work together to make this your most profitable year ever.

Michelle, as you suggested, I'll call you after your committee meeting, April 11, to discuss the next step you'd like to take.

Make doing business with you easy! Make it easy for them to give you their dollars and they'll be more likely to give them to you instead of to your competition! (This isn't brain surgery!) $

CHAPTER

6

THE CLEAN UP SPOT: REWRITE, REVISE, EDIT

"If you don't do your homework, you won't make your free throws."

— Larry Bird

"Good fortune is what happens when opportunity meets with preparation."

— Thomas Edison

Years ago, when I coached girls softball, we always saved one of the strongest batters for the seventh position. That way, when we had all the bases loaded (Dream, dream, dream!), our strong batter could bring everyone home.

You want to bring the message home—to their home. You have to sweep up. You have to clean up.

Reread what you wrote

Then make changes. Revise it. Edit it. Polish it.

29

Does it sound like your sales letter or proposal answers the questions:

Why am I writing?
What do I want to say?
What must I accomplish?
What action or reaction do I want from my reader?

Cross out the "so-what" stuff

If your reader has to think to himself, "so what," don't bet the house on getting the job or making the sale.

Writing is a simple three step process

Prewrite (two minutes) - Know your purpose for writing

Write (10-20 minutes) - Have a conversation with your reader

Revise (5-10 minutes) - Clean it. Edit. Polish. Perfect.

Everyone—no matter how often your never–been–in–the–Real–world English teacher reminded you how stupid you were in writing, and no matter how many times you had to rewrite your "What I did over my summer vacation" composition—everyone can write.

Relax and keep reading. $

MIXED MESSAGES: MAKE SURE YOU WILL NOT BE MISUNDERSTOOD

"The primary source of quality failure is miscommunication between the client and the professional."
— David Maister

Meanings lie in people—not words.

Meanings not only lie in the minds of the people reading and listening to your words, meanings lie! They mean one thing to me and one thing to you. My meaning is exceptionally clear to me and I can't imagine any one not understanding my message. It's so clear...to me!

Only once a week?

I was in the check out line at a Safeway grocery store in Phoenix. It was a Wednesday night (this is important to remember!) and all I wanted to do was run in, get the milk and run out. A new sign had recently been taped to the cash register: "No alcoholic beverages, beer or wine, sold until 10:00 am Sunday."

A woman in front of me was carrying a six pack of beer. I watched as she read, then reread the sign, looked at her beer and then read the sign one more time. Pointing to the sign, she asked the cashier why she would have to wait until Sunday at ten to buy her beer.

Spell that name please

I called a prospect the other day and he wasn't in. His assistant asked if he could take a message and I was delighted. "Yes," I said, "please ask him to call Sue back."

"Sure. How do you spell that?"

"What?"

"Suback."

If you cannot read this...

The seat back safety cards for United Airlines at one time said (in English, Chinese, Japanese, Spanish, French and German): "If you are sitting in an exit row and you cannot read this card, please tell a crew member." E–x–c–u–u–u–u–u–s–e me? This turned out to be an unbelievably expensive mistake, by the way.

United received so many comments about the wording that thirty days after putting those safety cards in every seat back of every seat on every plane, they removed the four color, heavy laminated over sized cards from every seat back of every plane, and replaced them with cards that read: "If you are sitting in an exit row and cannot understand this card..." My tiny little mind can't fathom how much it cost United to make that one word change.

Did you understand what I meant to say?

Metacommunications are ideas expressed and then interpreted differently than the sender intended. It's foot-in-mouth disease on a global scale! And it occurs much more often in sales writing than it does in sales talking.

When we talk to each other, whether it's over the phone, one on one, or even when we're giving a full blown sales presentation to a board of directors, senders (us, the sellers) and receivers (them, the buyers) give each other clues about receptivity of the idea, understanding of the situation, or boredom with the whole kit and caboodle. (When was the last time you heard that cliche?)

When we talk, if we're observant and sensitive to our buyers' expressions, voice tone and body language, we know when to backtrack, back down or back out of the room.

What we write may not be received right

In writing, we (the seller, the writer) receive no cues or clues from the reader. We don't know if our hot, hot prospect, who was so excited about our idea/solution/product/service when we met earlier, had just received news that his daughter is getting expelled from school, or if the project he has been nurturing for months finally had just received complete management approval!

Not only don't we know what frame of mind they'll be in (and we aren't there with our dynamic, charismatic, enthusiastic per-sonalities to lift them from their gloomy or inattentive spirits), we don't know how they'll read it (skim, check out the last page first, read only the first paragraph), when they'll read it, who else will be reading it with them and on and on and on.

The words are dead on the page/screen and open to *their* interpretation and *their* perception of reality. (Someone once said there is no reality, only our perception of it. Pretty heavy, huh?)

To be persuasive and powerful, it's critical to write not just so that your words will be understood. It's critical to write in a way that your words cannot possibly be misunderstood.

Reread the letter you wrote to Liz Lizbert and think about how else it can and may be interpreted.

What do these sentences mean to you?

I'll follow-up with you as soon as possible.

Sue's interpretation: It's January now. I guess they'll follow-up sometime before Passover and Easter. When is *as soon as possible*? I must not be a very important client to them. I guess they'll get to it whenever they get to it. Not what you meant? Then say what you mean!

Our new product line will be available world wide for spring distribution.

Sue's interpretation: Because I live in Australia, that must mean I can count on delivery in September. You did say spring, didn't you? Not what you meant? Then say what you mean!

If you have any additional questions, please do not hesitate to call me at any time.

Sue's interpretation: Really? So if I want to know if it's snowing in Scottsdale, I can call you at 3:00 a.m? You did say if I had any questions, I could call you at any time. Not what you meant? Then say what you mean!

Make it easy on the reader, say exactly what you mean

"Wait a minute, Sue. Aren't you taking this to the extreme? Who is going to think I mean what **you** think I mean?" Am I mind reading? Is that what you're thinking right about now? You're right. Most people don't have the same warped perspective that I have. I get paid big bucks to think about how other people might interpret your words.

They may not think exactly what I do, but they won't be thinking what you want them to, either! You will have placed a road block in the path of quick, clear understanding of your message.

Instead of making it easy to close the sale, instead of assuring them that you are focused on their best interests and creating a win-win partnership, you're throwing in little glitches.

Write it so clearly and plainly that you can feel confident they will interpret your words the way you want them to. 🕏

START WITH WHAT YOU WANT TO SAY—THIS ISN'T A MYSTERY NOVEL

"There are only two times to slowly build to a crescendo:

1. When it's vital your reader has a clear and complete picture of the value of your product/service/idea before you deliver the bad news, or

2. You're having really great sex."

— Sue A. Hershkowitz, CSP

I t's true. Some people write routine messages as if they're writing a musical composition that must slowly build to a crescendo. They think they're mystery novel writers and must provide all the clues before they get to the who-dun-it.

No, no, no!!! When you have good news to send or a routine message to give to your reader, <u>start with it</u>.

When would a sales person use this format?

• After you've visited with the client and he or she has asked you to send information

- After you've spoken on the phone and you're following-up

- After you have made some sort of contact and you have a routine, neutral message to send

Start with the news they're waiting to hear.

Great news! Your preferred dates are available at the rate we discussed for your 1999 meeting in Scottsdale.

Thanks for your time on the phone this morning. Here is the information I promised to send you. I'll follow-up with you Tuesday, January 13, to see how you would like to proceed.

I have reshipped your order of 10,000 widgets. They are scheduled to arrive June 16. The original order was shipped June 2. (A copy of the bill of lading is enclosed) I have placed a tracer on that shipment and I will follow-up with you the minute I hear from the shipping agent.

Your Platinum card status has been extended through December, 2001. We are delighted to make this exception for you.

Easy and efficient. Whenever you have a routine, neutral or good news message, begin with it.

When wouldn't you want to use this plan?

- When you need to sell!

Selling means you must grab their attention. You need to quickly get them to see what's in it for them; how they'll benefit, profit. When that is your purpose, this plan won't work. Use this plan when you are following up.

- When you have a negative message to send.

Don't use it when your reader will be upset by your information, stressed out, angry or anxious.

Again, start with the good stuff.

When your reader will be pleased with the information you have, or when the message you're presenting is routine or neutral, begin with the main idea. This is the perfect plan for following up, showing responsiveness or presenting information your reader is expecting or will be pleased to learn. ⑤

PART
II

FINE–TUNING YOUR
MESSAGE

Well, you've seen how easy it can be to start your communications and you've learned proven techniques to help you out of the procrastination, I–was–never–any–good–at– writing–stuff blues.

This section of the book will show you how to streamline your message. Whether it's knowing when and how to break the bad news, or determining if an apology is needed (or smart!) You'll learn critical ideas and power techniques to make your letters get the result you want.

The heart of good written communication is in knowing and understanding the reader. Read on to discover how easy it is to compel them to read your messages.

THE BUFFER ZONE: HOW TO SOFTEN BAD NEWS

"When written in Chinese, the word 'crisis' is composed of two characters—one represents danger, and the other represents opportunity."

— John F. Kennedy

"In calm water every ship has a good captain."

— Swedish Proverb

You can't begin a "negative" message with the negative news. (Pretty negative, huh?! Okay. I'll start again.)

Begin a negative message with something that allows your reader (buyer) to save face; something that shows appreciation for the reader or builds value into the situation. (Better? We'll talk more about "reframing" later in the book. Here is a teaser: You can expect response from your reader one–third more quickly when you present your information in a positive framework.)

Facing the bad news

Picture this. For the third time this week, and for the third week in a row, your most junior sales person walks into the office late. You are frustrated and furious. You get to her desk before she does and you begin the attack:

> "Eileen, you have been late three times this week. You have been late at least three days in each of the preceding three weeks. I have had enough. Either you are a part of this team, or you aren't." (You didn't really mean to give her an ultimatum, but you're angry.)

Stick around long enough to hear her reply and you might hear something like:

> "My car has been acting up" .."the baby is sick"..."have you seen the construction on the freeway? How do you expect me to get here on time? Pay me more and I'll buy a helicopter." Or maybe she says: "How come you haven't noticed I'm here every night until 6:45? Of course you wouldn't. You always leave by 5:15."

Eileen has been late all the times you said she was. And you forced her into responding the way she did. Remember that Fight or Flight phenomena we all learned about in Psych 101? When someone attacks us (physically or verbally) our first primitive initial reaction is to fight (get belligerent, justify, blame) or flee (deny, ignore). As any Aikido master will tell you (thank you, Tom Crum, for the lesson you taught me) the best way to "defend" yourself is to go with the energy instead of resisting/fighting it.

Eileen's best response would have been, "You're right. I'll be on time from now on. Here is the situation I've been dealing with and here are the three ideas I'm trying to put into place to take care of it. Do you have any additional suggestions for me to help me overcome these obstacles I'm faced with more quickly?"

How to get what you want from them even if you have bad news

Right now, however, we're not dealing with what <u>they</u> should have done to help you out. We're not discussing how <u>they</u> could have gotten the result they wanted more quickly. We're talking about how <u>you</u> can enhance your chances of getting them to respond to you in the manner you want...how you can increase your chances of getting the result (sale) you're after.

Instead of attacking Eileen, begin with a buffer—an area of mutual agreement. (Notice, I didn't suggest beginning with bull. I'm not looking for something so sweet and syrupy that everyone in the universe will agree with it. I'm not looking for flowery at all.)

By helping your reader to feel neutral or positive toward your message, and by giving him or her the opportunity to save face, whatever your eventual message turns out to be, you increase the likelihood of getting the response you desire.

Consider beginning with this buffer

Core hours here are eight to three thirty.

Compare that to:

Eileen, you've been late three times this week.

Which one would you stay more open to? Which one might you be more likely to continue to read? Remember (and this isn't going to be rocket scientist stuff):

If they don't read your message, you can't get the result you want. You need to write in a manner that will both encourage and motivate them to read because you, with your bright, shiny, enthusiastic face, aren't there to charm them into it!

Let's try another example

An important client sends you an idea he believes will help you save a great deal of money. Because you value his business and respect his business acumen, you discuss the idea with your team at your executive retreat. Been there, done that, you're told. Won't work. Forget it. How are you going to tell him?

Begin with a buffer!

```
Dear Mr. Important Client:

Thank you so much for sending
your idea to us. We really ap-
preciate the time you took to
write to us. (Buffer)
```

By allowing your reader to save face, you increase your chances of getting him or her to actually read your message.

What's next? Keep reading! $

CROSSING THE BRIDGE TO THE BAD NEWS...AND OVER TO THE SOLUTION (SALE)

Dear Mom and Dad:

*I'm writing on this school paper because my statio-
nery got lost in the fire. Just the other day, I got out
of the hospital and moved in with Bill my boyfriend.
Your new grandbaby is due next fall.*

Your loving daughter, Ellen

*P.S. None of the above is true. I did, however, make
a "D" in Chemistry and an "F" in Latin and I
wanted you to see this in its proper perspective.*

— Anonymous

O nce the buffer is in place, the next step is to move to the
transitional bridge. This bridge prepares your reader
(buyer) for the bad news. Before dumping the negative
or disappointing message on them, you bridge to the "bad" news
with **education**. You educate. You <u>sell</u> acceptance of your plan/
solution/idea.

Building the best bridge

The bridge shouldn't sound like those rejections from college, employment or credit, by the way! Remember receiving these: "Your application is one of the most impressive applications we've received in our office this week." ...and then what comes? "*However, but, I'm sorry...*" That is not what I'm suggesting!

Remember Eileen from the previous chapter? Here is the e-mail we can send her:

> Core hours here are eight to three thirty. *For the past three days, you've been coming in between 8:15 and 8:55.*

Remember Mr. Important Client's idea? Senior Management trashed it. We left off with the buffer. Here's the buffer and the bridge, or transition, into the bad news:

> Dear Mr. Important Client:
>
> Thank you so much for sending your idea to us. We really appreciate the time you took to write to us. *(Buffer)*
>
> *Your idea was discussed at our executive retreat. Our finance department had tried using the database you suggested earlier in the year. After a three month test, they*

> *recommended we continue using
> the All Comp software sys-
> tem. We will review this de-
> cision, look at upgrades and
> other packages at six month
> intervals. (Transitional bridge and nega-
> tive news)*

Notice how it isn't necessary to hit him over the head with another rejection statement. Nothing will be gained by adding: "We, therefore, cannot accept your idea."

Educate Some More!

You're cooking now. If possible, add additional education or provide an alternative solution. End friendly and on an upbeat note.

> Dear Mr. Important Client:
>
> Thank you so much for sending
> your idea to us. We really ap-
> preciate the time you took to
> write to us. *(Buffer)*
>
> Your idea was discussed at our
> executive retreat. Our fi-
> nance department had tried
> using the database you sug-
> gested earlier in the year.
> After a three month test, they
> recommended we continue using
> the All Comp software sys-
> tem. We will review this de-

cision, look at upgrades and other packages at six month intervals. *(Transitional bridge and negative news)*

Mr. Important Client, your ideas are very important to us. We understand that the only way we can truly serve your needs is to listen to what our customers tell us. Every idea we receive is thoughtfully evaluated and gratefully appreciated. *(Additional education)*

Again, thank you for thinking of us. We look forward to many, many years of serving your needs.

Sincerely,

Now, let's go back and finish dealing with Eileen's tardiness:

Eileen, core hours here are 8 a.m. to 3:30 p.m. For the past three days, you've been coming in between 8:15 and 8:55. I need you here during that entire time to be available to serve our customers the way we've promised them and to help the entire department run more smoothly.

What's the difference between the first "rejection" of Eileen and the second? Do you think I'd be more likely to get her to focus on the result I need (the sale - getting her to be at work in a timely manner) by getting her defensive or by using this negative news sales strategy?

Let's review:

- Begin with a buffer.

- Move to the transitional bridge, when needed.

- Present the "bad news" in objective, neutral or positive terms.

- Educate. Offer alternative solutions.

- End friendly and cooperatively.

Whenever you can't give the prospect or client whatever he or she is hoping for, use this plan. That's all there is to it. ⑤

GOOD WRITING MEANS NEVER HAVING TO SAY YOU'RE SORRY

"Laws are made to trouble people, and the more trouble they make, the longer they stay on the statute books."

— Finley Peter Dunne

"The first thing we do; let's kill all the lawyers."

— Shakespeare, Henry VI

"Lawyers are like beavers: They get in the mainstream and dam it up."

— John Naisbitt, Megatrends

Most of us were raised to believe if we said the "magic" words, "please," "thank you," and "I'm sorry," life would go on like a bowl of cherries. And that's true until we're about eight years old! Around eight, reality kicks in! When we apologize, tears and all, our mothers/fathers/teachers say, "Before I accept your apology, what will you do differently next time?"

Somehow we seem to forget that lesson and believe that if we say we're sorry to the client for the misunderstanding, if we say it often enough and appear to be heartfelt in our apology, they will say, "Okay...I know you didn't mean it. It's okay now. You can go outside and play." W–r–o–o–n–g!!!

The high cost of apologies

Apologies not only don't help the reader, they also can cause litigation and payouts.

John Doe (in case you're wondering, yes, the names are changed!) is on his way to work, and notices a defect in the tire of his wife's car. Because she has to drop the kids off on her way to work, John goes back into the house and graciously gives her his car to use.

Instead of going directly to work, John, driving his wife's car, with the defected tire he noticed earlier, stops at the tire store to take care of the problem. It looks funny to the 19–year–old tire "technician" too, and he generously replaces it for his customer.

By the time John gets to work, all heck has broken loose. Apparently, a customer who had been on the edge, called looking for John and when he wasn't in yet (that's what the secretary said) and when no one else seemed to know what the customer was ranting and raving about, he told them what they could do with their product.

John arrives late. In a fit of fury, is terminated by his supervisor who is sick and tired of John arriving late with a myriad of excuses. (Today, at least, it's original!)

With time on his hands, John writes the tire company a letter explaining the situation and the defect that started it. The tire company customer service person, somewhere along the line, learned that empathy was a good customer service strategy. She writes back to John, "I'm sorry about the defect you found in your tire" and then explains that, in fact, it wasn't a defect. It was a very natural process in the rubber that the service station didn't explain properly.

John sued the tire company for loss of income. They settled, out of court, for $20,000. Not a huge amount from the tire company's perspective, but why did it happen? Because someone put in black and white: "I'm sorry about the defect..."

I was telling that story at an international hotel company I work with and the director of national sales practically jumped out of his seat and yelled, "We are undergoing identical litigation."

Nothing had ever been put in writing. The hotel sales associate said she told a corporate meeting planner that she would hold a block of sleeping rooms for him for three weeks. She held the rooms in his name for three weeks and then released them.

Two months later, he phoned, wanting those rooms. (To make this even worse, he had been sick and hospitalized for part of the time.) Because of a citywide convention coming to Chicago, the room block he wanted, was not to be found. He called her back and was verbally abusive toward her. Not wanting to lose his future business, she sent him a public relations type of letter. She wrote, "I'm sorry I didn't hold the block of rooms for you. I should have phoned you before releasing them."

Bingo! Pivotal point that the case went to court on. (Still in the courts—and both companies are losing money and energy over it.)

What can you do besides, to paraphrase Shakespeare, kill all the lawyers?

Stop apologizing in your sales letters for anything. Start focusing on the <u>solution</u>.

My company was exhibiting at a trade show being held in a major New York City hotel. They had very strict show rules. One rule required that all printed material be docked into the warehouse within a window of 10 - 14 days prior to the event or they would not distribute it to the booth at the show. Knowing the sheer number of people who come and go from that hotel during that time period, I was sure my stuff would get lost. Besides, I was very low on printed matter.

I called a printing company in NYC who promised to drop ship my printing to my booth at the show. The appointed time, 10:00 a.m., came and went. No printing. I called the company and no one was able (capable?) of locating my order. (No one could locate my sales rep either, naturally.)

At 1:00 p.m., the show doors opened and my printing rep came rushing in, profusely apologetic. He was so sorry. He was so sorry. He was so sorry, but they had a press breakdown and he wasn't able to get me my printing.

What was the only thing in the entire world that mattered to me at that moment? My printing.

What did his apology do for me? Nothing!

What did his apology do for him? Everything! It made him

feel better, eased his conscience and guilt.

What I wanted and what the people you work with want as well, is a focus on the solution, not the apology. I wanted to know when he was going to get me my printing. When he would get me black and white work instead of the four color I ordered. How he was going to compensate me for having to put his late printed pieces into envelopes with (expensive) stamps.

Forget the apology in writing

Focus on the solution. The customer service issue is your responsiveness to the customer/client—not your ability to grovel.

How can you make it right? What can you do right then, at that moment, to take care of the situation? Figure it out and do it. That's the making of legendary customer service. Saying I'm sorry, isn't. 💲

WHEN THE READER IS RIGHT, USE AIKIDO IN WRITING

"Maybe, if I ask you how things look to you, and you ask me, between us we'll see something we never saw before."
— The Jewish Theological Seminary of America
- High Holiday Message

"If you could only love enough, you could be the most powerful person in the world."
— Emmett Fox

The principles of Aikido, as I understand them, are to go with the source of the energy, in the same direction as the movement. By moving in the direction the energy is flowing, the attacker is actually thrown off balance and the attacked gains control. In Aikido, the point is to hurt no one. The goal is to simply disable your attacking opponent (until he or she sees your point of view!).

Writing and Aikido have much in common. When you attempt to resist or refute the other person, you often lose.

Aikido at the airport

My parents live in Tucson, AZ. Tucson has a relatively small airport and traffic on the way to the airport is practically nonexistent. My parents "summer" in San Diego. (Sounds fancy, huh? Actually, they do this elder hostel thing and live in a college dorm!)

Last Father's Day, I decided to fly into San Diego to spend the day with them. Unprepared for the traffic they encountered, they got to the San Diego airport a bit late. They couldn't find a parking spot, but my dad spotted a young couple wheeling a luggage cart. He followed them and stopped immediately when they did. He knew that parking spot had his name on it. What he didn't realize, was that he had stopped right in the middle of the traffic lane. No one could get around him in either direction.

To make matters worse, the couple with the luggage cart were in no rush whatsoever. My father was very patient. He knew he would, eventually, get the spot.

The car that pulled up behind my father, well, that was a different story. Unable to get around him, they were not feeling kindly at all! They started honking their horn to get my father to move. They honked and honked. My father didn't budge—that parking space was his.

Exasperated, the woman passenger got out of the car, stomped over to my father's window and shouted "You old people, you shouldn't even be driving."

My dad looked right at her. "You're right," he said. "We shouldn't."

That was it! What was she going to say? "You're right, I'm right. I've never been so right!"

My dad said her jaw dropped and she looked back at him. A moment later, she marched back to her car (and probably had a fight with the man who made her get out in the first place!)

Admit the reader is right, then center on the solution

When you're wrong, when you've over promised and under delivered, the best way to communicate is to write, "You're right and..." and then focus on the **solution** or on how you'll atone.

Do not, did you hear that, do not write: "You're right, <u>but</u>..." What is the metacommunication of "you're right, but..."? (You've never been right a day in your life, why oh why would you start today, buster!) Keep the "buts" out of your way.

Think about how you can help your reader (buyer) save face. Make it easy for them to give you the result you want. Make it pleasant for them to do business with you. $

THE CONVERSATIONAL TEST: UNLESS YOU'RE WILLIAM F. BUCKLEY, THERE'S NO NEED TO USE BIG WORDS

"In baiting a mousetrap with cheese, always leave room for the mouse."

— Saki

Have you ever noticed how nice normal people turn into the "Man from Webster's" when they write? It's a riot!

For some reason, intelligent people switch form their normal, conversational, rapport–building style of communicating, to an uncomfortable, stuffy, pompous and unattached style.

What's up with this?

All voice mail messages will be accompanied with complete directions on the retrieval of your message, and options to save or delete any messages through depressing the 5 5 keys on your telephone keypad. *(Word for word directions for hotel message system use.)*

What is with that? Did they mean:

Please touch 55 to retrieve your voice messages.

Or:

You can hear directions for retrieving your voice messages by touching 55.

Do we really need to beef up our language?

Back in 1983, The Wall Street Journal ran an article called, "Conversation: The Key to Better Writing." Here is an excerpt:

> Why does the man who seems so direct and clear on the phone make himself sound mechanical, pompous and stilted in his writing? First, he is probably insecure about his writing skills. He doesn't trust his own use of language enough to write naturally. And he thinks that somehow jargon, wordy expression, the passive voice and puffy sentences will make him appear more educated or more polished than he fears he really is. Second, he may be under the impression that business writing is supposed to seem stuffy, roundabout and impersonal since so many of the memos he gets read that way. ...All of these reasons are equally bad.

Why is "Man from Webster" so common? People think they need to dress up their writing because they always had to do it in school. Remember those horrible 150–word compositions? It didn't matter if you said everything you needed to say in 50 words, did it? Your teacher said 150 and you had to keep going.

"Teacher, does 'a' count as a word? How about 'the'?" When we got to 150, some of us would just stop. (You know who you are - you're the ones laughing right now!) Hey, why not...we met the criteria, didn't we?! Why go on?

In college, it got even worse. Remember filling in those Blue Books? We knew if we could write enough to complete a Blue Book, we were guaranteed a "B." If we said anything good, we might even get an "A!"

How did you write your first business letter?

With graduation, we finally get out into the world of work. Very quickly, someone tells us to put our ideas in writing and we realize, we don't know how!

What do most of us do? We go to the files—and using the Joe Biden School of Copying as a model—we copy what someone else wrote! What we don't realize is that we're copying from someone who had copied form someone else, five years earlier who, had copied from someone else five years earlier.....

If you reread your letters, memo, e-mail, two weeks after you wrote them and they don't sound like you wrote them, this is a good clue for you that you're not writing conversationally.

Write as if you are face–to–face with your reader

Write like you would talk to your reader if you were in the same situation. Everything you write should be aimed toward building rapport and relationships, credibility and confidence. Do it by being you. ❸

CHAPTER

14

FOCUS ON YOUR READER TO EARN DOLLARS QUICKLY

"There can be no friendship without confidence, no confidence without integrity."
— Samuel Johnson

D o you think you could talk to a colleague/life partner/ child/ manager/client for three minutes or more and not use the pronoun "I?" My money is on the table. Go ahead, make my day. If you can't do it, just send me $5.00 in a plain brown wrapper! If you did it, try talking for two minutes longer!

Ninety eight per cent of the adult American population can't talk for five minutes or longer without referring to themselves. (I have no research on this, but I would bet that 98% of the French population can't talk without using "Je", and Spanish speaking people can't talk without using "Yo" (neither can people from the Bronx—ha!) and that people who speak Farsi can't do it without saying I/me in Farsi....

It's easiest, of course, to talk in terms of our own experiences. We're most comfortable.

So why do I use "I" and "me" so often?

You know why we really can't talk without talking about our-selves, our experiences, our thoughts? WE ARE SELF-CEN-TERED! SELFISH! EGOCENTRIC! (Only 98% of us are. I'm not talking to the other 2% of you!)

Most of us write in a self-centered manner too.

> I would like to take this oppor-tunity to introduce myself to you. My name is Marvin Marvelous and I am the new sales manager at Treetop Lumber. Formerly with Woodpecker Lumber, I have been selling lumber packages for many years.
>
> I have been involved in the lum-ber and home building industry since 1978. My experience in-cludes working with contractors, architects, and in the field. Bob Harton, your previous sales man-ager is no longer with us.
>
> Please replace Harton's card with mine and call me whenever you are in need of a quality lumber package at fair cost.
>
> We do it right here at Treetop.

Save it for your mother! She is the only one who cares about all those credentials.

Focus your letter on what's in it for the reader

Dear Paul,

"Thank you for finally providing us with a package with no twisted or unusable lumber. You charge a fair market price and then give us good value. We save money every time we order from you. We'll be opening a new subdivision soon. Count on us to keep reordering."

Frank Franklin;
Global Builders

Treetop Lumber has been helping major home builders, like Global, save money and provide the highest quality lumber to their home owners for 18 years.

Bob Horton, your former sales manager with Treetop, has relocated. He and I have reviewed your specs. Please feel confident that with my knowledge of your account combined with my fifteen years of experience in the lumber industry, I will continue to provide you with

> the seamless, high quality
> service you expect from Tree-
> top.
>
> I will phone you, November
> 12, to set up a time when it
> will be convenient for you
> to review your upcoming
> needs.
>
> Looking forward to working with
> you!
>
>   Sincerely,
>   Marvin

Someone once said: It doesn't matter how much you know until they know how much you care about their needs. It's a great line.

Do you remember reading Dale Carnegie's excellent book, <u>How to Win Friends and Influence People</u>. (If you haven't read it in a few years, buy a new copy or borrow it from your library.) Carnegie tells a story that I'm going to modify a bit:

> I love hot fudge. I mean I really love hot fudge. It stands to reason, if I were to go fishing, that I would squish a piece of fudge and put it on the hook. Why not? If I saw that piece of fudge dangling, I'd bite!! If the fish sees the fudge dangling, it will probably look up and think: "This lady is crazy!"

If I want to catch that fish, I better put something on that hook that will be interesting/enticing/seductive to that fish! If I use a kernel of corn, or a piece of bread, or (yuck!) a minnow, I'm more likely to get what I want.

I wish I had a dollar for every time good, effective sales people forget this basic Sales 101 technique when they write. It's like taking money that belongs in your pocket and letting it fly away in the breeze. The sale is there for you...and because you don't focus on them and their needs, it's blown.

Find out about your reader (customer)

I was conducting a sales rally for a group of real estate professionals recently, and a woman in the group told how she had picked up a 1.4 million dollar home. A prospective customer phoned three real estate professionals to say she was selling her home and that she would interview each of them. After meeting with all three, she would make a decision.

My audience member was number three. She looked at the woman's house, chatted a bit about how lovely it was (normal stuff) and allowed the seller to talk all about how much money she wanted to make, etc. When she was done, the real estate professional said, "May I ask you why you're selling your home?" The woman looked at her, grew very quiet, and said, "Bring me your agreement. I want you to represent me."

What had happened? The other two agents were so wrapped up in getting square footage and so concerned with altering curb appeal, and so involved in getting her to clean her closets that they never asked why she was selling the home. They assumed divorce when, in fact, the husband had died. The woman in my sales rally was selected because she simply asked why she was doing it before she told her how she would do it.

Sales people get so driven by their own agendas (the great things they have to offer and the great need to make the sale) they forget to focus on why the buyer is buying! They forget to write about how what they have will meet (exceed) their (buyers) needs, objectives, or goals of making them happier/richer/more professional/ more productive/safer/smarter/and more sane!

Focusing on their needs doesn't mean thinking for them.

I was working in San Juan, Puerto Rico and I took an extra day there to play. Flipping through their tourist magazine, <u>Que Pasa, What's Happening</u>, I noticed an ad for the Rain Forest, a major tourist attraction. The ad read:

> You will not leave our beautiful rain forest without eating a delightful lunch at our new tropical restaurant.

You will not leave? I got this great picture of people standing at the edge of the Rain Forest questioning each person as he or she is leaving: "Did you eat? You didn't? Get back in there, you!"

We can't think for another person. Yet, I often see over eager sales people write things like:

- You will benefit from... (How do you know?)

- You'll be excited to hear about... (That's not what excites me, really!)

Forget the golden rule

Yes, that's right. Forget it. The Golden Rule says, "Do unto others as you would have them do unto you." Do that and you're likely to do what makes you happy instead of them.

An elevator is a great example. Have you ever noticed when you're riding on an elevator how there is absolute silence and everyone stands there staring at the numbers..9....10....11.... as if it's the most fascinating thing in the world. I find this really boring, so I start conversations. Those elevator doors open, and passengers are out of there, whether it's their floor or not!

I've realized that I can't do what I want—carry on a conversation. I have to do what they (buyers) want and that is— shut up!

Another example. A few years ago I booked a speaking engagement to speak on Valentine's Day in Denver. When I booked it I asked my son, Michael, 15 at the time, if he would like to go up with me. I figured we could drive to the mountains and ski all weekend. Yes, yes, he'd love to go. For three months we talked about this ski trip. The Thursday before the Saturday of the trip, Michael comes home from school, asking if the ski trip, is in fact, that weekend.

> "Yes, honey, we've been talking about it for three months."

> "Oh," he said, "Then I guess I shouldn't have invited anyone to the Valentine's Dance Saturday night."

> "You invited someone? What did she say?"

> "Yes."

> "Yes?"

And then for the next ten minutes, I screamed at him. Couldn't believe how selfish he was, I told him, after I had made all those plans for us, after I had made special arrangements to get the room, after I had done this and that...

"All right, Ma, we'll go," he said after I piled on
the guilt pretty deep.

"You're darn right, we're going to go," I fumed.
(And we're going to have fun!)

Only I couldn't sleep that night. I stayed awake thinking that
my teen age son had the opportunity to spend the entire weekend with his mother, or he could go on a date with a woman
who had already said yes. Let's see....mother...date! It wasn't brain
surgery!

The next morning I told him I had been thinking about it and
if we stayed home, I'd actually save money and I'd have some
time to relax. He could go to the dance.

"You're kidding, Ma, you'd do that?"

And I need to explain why I did it. I didn't do it because I'm
such a wonderful mother (I wish that were true!). I did it because
I've learned that we "teach" best that which we most need to
learn. For years I've used this concept as the foundation of both
my sales writing classes and my customer service workshops. I've
always stressed, "Focus on their agenda ...Look at it from their
point of view... Drive it through their needs."

And there I was focusing only on what I wanted and what I
did and what I knew.

The interesting thing is that by looking at it from my customer's
(son's!) point of view, I got just what I wanted—quality time together.

The moral of these stories?

If you want to use your writing to make more dollars, focus the proposal, focus all your information on their needs, objectives, and agenda.

If you're a hotelier, don't bother telling them about the 49 varieties of palm trees you have in your atrium area (unless you're selling to the National Association of Arborists!). They don't care. You do.

If you're a real estate professional, don't tell them how successful you've been selling homes in a different price bracket. They won't care. Tell them what your marketing plan is for them based on their needs.

Focusing on the reader's agenda is a win–win situation. ⑤

UNDERSTAND WHAT MATTERS TO YOUR READERS

"If people around you will not hear you, fall down before them and beg their forgiveness, for in truth you are to blame."

— Fyodor Dostoyevsky

If you were having elective surgery and your doctor agreed to go with you to any hospital in your area, but for liability reasons, would not give a recommendation, how would you go about selecting your hospital? Would you base your decision on what your friends thought? (What if they had a different set of expectations than you?) Would you call the American Medical Association and conduct research? Would you visit the hospital to see how clean it is? Would you walk around to get a "feel" for the hospital? Would you count them going in and count them going out (and whether they were upright or in the permanently prone position)?

Six thousand people, all having been patients within the prior six months, were asked how they would, in the future, select a hospital. Turned out they had two significant answers.

1. Service. This had to be defined since service to one person means something different than it does to the next. Service had two components:

a. Nurses had to be friendly. (Friendly was defined as smiling appropriately)

b. Nurses had to be attentive.

The number two reason for selecting a hospital blew me away! No, not food.

2. Parking. Yes! Parking! It makes perfect sense after a moment of thought. Sick people want visitors and how can I ask you to come visit me if I know you'll have to pay ten dollars for the hour? How can I ask you to visit me if I know that when you leave you'll have to walk through a very unsafe neighborhood?

Parking! I know this sounds crazy but this is exactly what this chapter is about. No, not about me being crazy, but about looking at our services/products/solutions from the reader's/customer's perspective.

When you write, don't bother to tell them, for example, if you run a trasportation company, that you can transport them to their destination safely. Yes, it matters to them, but they figured that! Tell them how you can enhance return on investment; how you can make a difference on their expense account; how you can increase their productivity; make their jobs easier and more enjoyable.

Tell them what's in it for them

Answer the reader's "so what" questions and you'll be writing sales letters extraordinaire!

Years ago when I got into the speaking business a colleague of mine, Joe Charbonneau, CSP, CPAE, told me to list at least ten features I bring to the platform. (This was very difficult at that time...I didn't know what I was selling let alone what they might be buying...any of you feel that way about what you sell?)

Features

For you newbies, features are qualities you/your products/solution have. They are neither good nor bad, they just are. A coffee maker in my hotel room is a feature the hotel offers. It's not good and it's not bad. If I hate coffee, it's of no benefit to me to have it on my bathroom vanity. In fact, it may be an inconvenience because it takes away valuable space on that vanity. If I must have a cup of freshly brewed coffee in the morning even before I brush my teeth, that coffee maker not only becomes a benefit, it's a blessing.

Go ahead, take a minute (or ten minutes, or three months like it took me!) and list ten unique (if possible) features of the services/solutions/products you sell.

Take each item on your feature list and add five benefits to your buyer. (If you want to do this later, okay. But do it!)

Now you have the keys to your success strategy

Once you discover what about your solution/service/product matters to them, you can easily write a benefit–laden sales proposal/letter.

If you're writing an unsolicited direct mail piece, use your strongest benefit, the one most people ask you about, most often and lead off with that. See how simple this is!

Here is an honest-to-goodness direct response letter written by a hotel sales person. (Keep in mind that if it is a direct response letter, your purpose is to get a response!) My comments are within the brackets < >.

Dear Association Executive:

Association business is extremely important to the We Want You Hotel. <How self centered can you get? Who cares what type of business is important to you?> ...therefore it is my pleasure <again, who cares what your pleasure is!> to introduce you to the hotel in the hope we may have an opportunity to host one of your groups. <and one more time no concern about me, the association exec..only concern about you and that you may have the opportunity to make money off of one of my groups>.

Located in downtown San Francisco and just steps away from Union Square shopping, the Cable Cars and the Financial District, the We Want You Hotel (WeWe) offers easy access to an abundance of activities. <Is this your most important feature..that you are located close to an abundance of activities? Is easy access the benefit? If this matters to the Association Executive, then focus on what they can gain by being within close proximity to all those activities.> Inside, the hotel accommodates groups with over 1,000 sleeping rooms and 18,000 square feet of meeting space. Enclosed is a brochure and floor plan for your library. <The fact that you have as a feature many sleeping rooms means nothing to me...what is the benefit? If I am an association executive from a small association, like the coffee pot example, I will find this to be an inconvenience because my group will be only a small fish in a big pond. If, on the other hand, my association requires 1,000 rooms so we can all be in the same hotel for better networking, smoother running meetings, now your numbers become a benefit.>

Thank you for your consideration

```
of our property  <Who said they
considered anything?  Property?
This may be hotel talk but how
comfortable is the buyer with
this terminology?>.  If I may be
of assistance, I invite you to
phone me at (555)555-5555. <Are
you selling or telling?  Take
responsibility for following up.>
I will look forward to assisting
you in the near future. <When
exactly is the "near future?">

Best Regards,  <Try Sincerely >
```

Now would you like to know how I really feel about it??

Now it's your turn

Take the time to rewrite this letter. Remember it is a direct response piece. You are selling. You make your living making sales. Your time is money. (This is a hint!)

Of course, the first thing you did before you rewrote the letter was ANSWER THE FOUR PRE-WRITING QUESTIONS!

Why am I writing?

To get them interested enough in my hotel that they will accept my phone call

What do I want to say?

Your members will save time and money because of our unbelievable location—lots of space to accommodate all your attendees under one roof to further networking and smoother running meeting; great access for after meeting activities.

What do I want to accomplish?

I want them to consider using WeWe for their next year's meeting (Be specific here) I also want to find out more about their meeting history and start building a relationship.

What action or reaction do I want as soon as my reader finishes reading?

I want them to understand I'll be following up with them on a specific date to set up a site inspection. I want them interested enough to accept my phone call.

Dear Association Executive:

AFTER A SUCCESSFUL DAY'S MEETINGS...EASY ACCESS TO SAN FRANCISCO'S ATTRACTIONS...

Your attendees work hard at their meetings all day and when it's time to gather them to visit San Francisco's famous sights, the WeWe hotel is the perfect choice.

Experienced with association groups such as yours, WeWe has 1,000 beautifully appointed sleeping rooms--enough to house all of your delegates under one roof. Being together, they will not only experience

---

greater networking opportunities, your meetings will just
naturally flow more smoothly.
And when the work is done...

Your attendees can hop on a
cable car and shop, shop, shop
at Union Square (just steps
away!), visit the famed Financial District, and get back to
their home away from home, safely
and quickly for another productive day of meetings.

WeWe has so much to offer to
make your next meeting a huge
success. I'll phone you, April
11 to discuss your specifica-
tions and to invite you to visit
our beautiful hotel.

Sincerely,

Focus on what matters to them

Understand their needs and why you're writing. Let your letters do your selling for you. $

REFRAME: ACCENTUATE THE POSITIVE

"As he thinketh in his heart, so is he."
— Proverbs 23:7

"Experience is not what happens to a man; it is what a man does with what happens."
— Aldous Huxley

"All that is necessary to break the spell of inertia and frustration is this: Act as if it were impossible to fail."
— Dorothea Brande

Reframing is one of my favorite strategies for getting results. Fast. So few people do it and yet we have statistical evidence that when you reframe—when you format a message in a positive manner—you get response one–third more quickly than had you written the same information in a negative framework.

You get response (from your buyer - read money, profits, rich) one–third more quickly.

Say want you want them to do not what you DON'T want

When you present negative messages, negatively, you get your reader to think of what you don't want them to do instead of what you do want from them.

I was working in a publishing plant in Kingsport, TN. Along the plant wall they had signs, every five feet apart, that said, "Don't run...don't run...."   Walking with the VP, I turned and said, "Excuse me, but do those signs mean that you would like me to walk? "Of course," he said. "Then," I suggested,"How about having them read, 'Walk, please!'"

Tell them what you do want, what you can do, what criteria still needs to be met instead of what you don't want, can't do, or don't have.

Normally when I drive, I speed. (If there are any law officers reading this, I drive the speed limit in your town. If my parents are reading this, this is only a joke. If my son is reading this, this is a lie. Drive safely, your life depends on it.) What I do is spend my time speeding, and paying attention, not to the road, but keeping one eye behind me, looking for the police car, one eye ahead of me looking for radar, and that leaves about half (or less) of an eye to do what I should be doing and that is driving safely.

Driving in New Mexico, however, changed my normal pattern. Every eight or ten miles, they had signs that read: *"Keep it at 55! You're saving money and gas!" "Keep it at 55. Get there alive!" "Keep it at 55. Get home to see your family tonight."* (This one may not have been as motivational as they intended!)

Every time I read one of those signs, I checked my speedometer and slowed down! Why not? They made perfect sense and they told me what I should be doing, not what I shouldn't.

Joel Weldon, CPAE, a motivational speaker says "Success comes in cans, not in can nots!"

Keep it positive
Instead of:

> We cannot process your application until our credit department has completed a search of your records,

try:

> As soon as our credit department completes your record search, your application can be processed, or: Your application will be processed as soon as our credit department completes their research.

Instead of:

> Your preferred dates of July 4 - 8 are not available,

try:

> Both July 7-10 and June 27-30 are available for your meeting. We can place a hold on the July 4th weekend for your meeting next year; this year July 4-6 is completely booked.

Is it easy to reframe messages?

Heck, no! According to the Zig Ziglar foundation, 84% of our adult communications are negative. Eighty four percent of what we hear each day, say each day and read each day, is negative. (Then we wonder why we have sour relationships with so many people!)

Present information in a positive, proactive way. This doesn't mean you have to act like that Saturday Night Live motivational character, "I'm great....) It does mean you need to consciously and conscientiously go out of your way to present the positive chunk, to tell them what is possible rather than what isn't.

The first step to effective reframing, by the way, is to start with your selling strategy. Under promise and over deliver and you will always be the bearer of good news!

When Michael was in the fifth grade, he came running home from school. His eyes were lit with excitement. The fifth grade choir was going to be singing on the steps of the newly opened Hyatt Gainey Ranch in Scottsdale, in two weeks. I ran to my calendar and I was booked - in New Orleans.

I called the client and told him he had my commitment and that I'd be at his meeting. I wondered, however, if he might be able to change the time of my one–hour presentation and I told him the reason.

The man should have been sainted. He had to print an inset for the program anyway and he had three kids of his own. He understood. He called the other speaker, made the changes, printed the program change, arranged for a car to pick me up from the hotel.

The date came and the presentation went perfectly. The car was waiting for me and I got to the New Orleans airport on time. Everything went like clockwork.

I arrived at the Dallas/Fort Worth airport to change planes and my connection was leaving on time. Leaving on time! I called Michael to tell him how excited I was that I would be there to see him sing. "One thing, though, remember to ask grandma and grandpa to get there early to save me a seat in the front row because I'm going to be rushing in," I said. (I had a twenty minute window.) "If they don't leave early enough to get me a seat, I'll be squished in the back."

"Gotta go, honey. They're calling final boarding. Love you. See you soon." I hung up the phone and rushed onto the plane. They closed the door right behind me, pushed back from the gate. But the plane didn't leave. It sat on that tarmac for two hours and twenty minutes. No phones on the plane yet. No recourse.

When we finally did get up in the air, two hours and twenty minutes later, and the flight attendant asked me if I preferred chicken or beef, I became hysterical crying. (She thought it was over the food selection!)

Get ready to soul search: Have you ever over promised and under delivered? Have you ever acted as if you were in control of a department that you really had absolutely no control over? If you're human, and if you're a professional salesperson, the answer has to be "yes!"

What should I have done? I should have under promised and, if possible, over delivered. I should have told Michael the truth. I should have explained that I would do everything possible to be there to see him sing. I should have been up front about my inability to control the exact time the plane would leave or what the weather might be (Can I really control another department's work schedule? I might want to...).

I should have acknowledged the plan - and admitted that the plan had not always worked perfectly in the past. I should have explained that there was a possibility that I might not make it. I should have developed an alternate plan - just in case, just in case, I wasn't there. (I could have asked my parents to video tape the program and told Michael that no matter what time I got home, I'd wake him up so I could see him sing on the steps of the Hyatt Gainey Ranch.)

It is so much easier for us, as sales people, to avoid the discussion of contingency plans. Why even put it in their minds is the thinking. It is so much easier for us to promise delivery of the printing at 4:00 p.m. (that's when they want it and we'll really, really do our best to get it there then) and then ask forgiveness when we get it to them at 6:00 p.m. But how do you keep them satisfied after that? How do you maintain their trust?

Under promise and over deliver. Promise big and deliver bigger. Communicate what you will do - not what you hope to do. Communicate what you can do - not what you can't.

Let's try it out

Earlier today you promised your CEO/sales manager/customer that you weren't exactly sure, but you thought you would be able to get her the price and the product she wanted. (Based on history, it wasn't unreasonable that you could swing the deal.) You made the appropriate phone calls, and just found out that because of some new price increases and demands, you cannot do what you said you thought you could. You look at the clock and you realize you've missed her. She is now on her way to Istanbul. You have to fax her a letter/memo so it is waiting for her at her hotel. Go for it!

Of course, the first thing you did was ANSWER THE FOUR PRE-WRITING QUESTIONS!!!

Why am I writing?

To offer alternate solutions

What do I want to say?

Here are three possible options for what we talked about

What do I want to accomplish?

Show leadership ability; show that I'm focused on solving her problem; show responsiveness; get her to consider another proposal

What action or reaction do I want as soon as my reader finishes reading?

Fax me back with an authorization to go ahead with one of my plans or to look into another option

(Many people initially think the reason they're writing is to let the reader know what they can't do.)

Dear Jennifer,

Hope your trip to Istanbul was restful and productive and that you accomplished all that work you had planned!

I checked into the rates and product that you and I discussed and I can discount the Raspberry Ice to .23 a dozen and the Blueberry Ice to .26 a dozen. The factory has significantly upgraded the materials they are using and has changed their supplier to ensure the on-time delivery of your product.

I called the Ice and Ice distributor directly and received price quotes from him of .23 and .24. He will guarantee only approximate dates for product delivery if the order adds up to fewer than 144 pieces. If the order is larger than 144, he will guarantee a two day window for delivery.

Because your reputation is on the line (and mine!), I recommend ordering from the original vendor. I will be happy to work out all the details from here and confirm, by fax, prices, delivery, etc.

To make it easy for you, please simply initial this memo and I will take care of all aspects of this for you. If I receive this back within 24 hours, I can have the order completed before you return from Istanbul.

Safe travels and a productive, profitable meeting!

Sincerely,

Sue

How did you do?

Reframe your message to help your reader give you the result you want. $

PART

III

MAKING THE SALE

Many of you already know the fine points of making a sale, but maybe you're not having too much luck translating those skills on paper.

If you want to learn how to capture your reader's attention within *five* seconds, or the best way to ask for the action— don't miss this section.

Making Money from Your Direct Mail Sales Letters

"If we really understand the problem, the answer will come out of it, because the answer is not separate from the problem."
— Krishnamurti

"Give me a lever long enough and a prop strong enough. I can single handedly move the world."
— Archimedes

Five seconds. One...two...three...four... five... That's it folks. Five seconds is all the time you have to capture your reader's (buyer's) attention when you're sending a direct mail piece.

Show the readers how they will benefit

They don't know you. They may not care to know you. How will you get them to read your money saving, money making, value laden proposition? There is only one way: Write about them and what they stand to gain.

Convince the reader to buy your product

First consider why you're writing. What do you want to accomplish by sending a direct mail piece? (These questions should sound vaguely familiar!) The reason you are sending the letter is to get them to buy or consider buying your product/service.

Open with a headline

Grab their attention immediately. Begin with an important message/invitation directed toward that buyer.

David Ogilvy, the immensely successful advertising whiz, in his book, <u>Confessions of an Advertising Man</u>, said, "The headline is the most important element...It is the telegram which decides whether the reader goes on to read the copy."

Five times more people will read the headline than the copy. Intrigue them with your headline and you have a fighting chance of getting them to read your sales letter.

Every headline must:

• Promise a benefit and arouse curiosity.

Why should I take my valuable time to read what you have just written to me. If you bore me and we're sitting next to each other at a luncheon meeting, I'll be polite. If you phone me, I'll listen until I can find a courteous way to disengage. Write to me, sucker, and you're on my time. Tell me about you—and you're history! Tell me about me and how I'll benefit and maybe I'll pay some attention. Maybe. I'm busy, you know. Promise me I can achieve something and you'll make it easier for me to do what you want me to do - read about your offer!

Here are some examples:

> <u>To meeting professionals from a speaker</u>:
> If your neck is on the line every time you hire a speaker, this information may, forever, dramatically change the way you select speakers...

> <u>To a homeowner from a landscaper</u>:
> Would it be worth a few dollars a month to have your yard look like a designer showplace and be a great, safe place for your children to play?

> <u>To a home seller from a real estate professional</u>:
> Save my commission with these three guaranteed home selling ideas....(of course, after providing these substantive ideas, you'd offer them five more ideas if they would call or send back the enclosed coupon; or you'd be happy to drop off a pamphlet with ten more ideas....and then, once you get to speak to them...)

Be specific.

Words like, *best in the world, absolutely lowest prices, greatest* (you fill in the blank!) are usually more damaging to the sale than helpful. You raise expectations to a level almost impossible to achieve. And you weaken your credibility with the reader. If you are the *best in the world*, surely you can be more specific about what you have achieved and what that means to me (the buyer).

Accentuate the positive:

> Paris is beautiful
> in the
> the spring time.

Did you see the two "the's"? Most people blast through that example so quickly they miss it. Most of us skim. We don't read! If you tell them what you can't do, rather than what you can, because they're skimming so quickly, they may very well misread your entire message. Try these:

- Our hotel does not charge extra for meeting room space.

- You will not be paying higher prices for our services.

- Our products contain no additives.

- The flowers you buy from us are guaranteed to not die.

Your reader may not even see the negative and will be left with:

- Our hotel does charge extra for meeting room space.

- You will pay higher prices for our services.

- Our products contain additives.

- The flowers you buy from us are guaranteed to die.

Say what you mean.

- Meeting Room space is complimentary.

- Our services are included.

- These products are pure, fresh and clean.

- These flowers will last, with proper care, for seven – ten days.

Be believable

This headline was tested by a vocational school:

"To Men and Women Who Want to Work Less
and Earn More"

It failed. Miserably. It brought in negligible response because nobody believed it could be true! Honesty goes a long way....

Use your five seconds wisely

Grab your reader's attention by using a specific positive, believable benefit-laden headline. If you're going to get results, you have to begin by getting attention. 🕲

Let the Reader Know What Others Think: Use Testimonials

"The principle of social proof: We determine what is correct by finding out what other people think is correct."

— Robert Cialdini, Influence

A few years ago I was putting together a program on marketing for colleagues of mine in the National Speakers Association. I faxed about 50 meeting professionals to find out why they were likely to hire us—or not. One particular question asked them to identify the method they used most often in selecting speakers. I listed a bunch of reasons for them to choose from, including:

• Author

• Industry expert

• Referrals

• Proven platform experience

It was a great list filled with logical reasons to select a speaker.

Word–of–mouth is still the strongest recommendation

Overwhelmingly, they told me they didn't select speakers because of beautiful brochures, videos, platform experience or fine credentials. They based decisions on whether someone they knew, liked and respected had heard a speaker speak and what they thought of them: <u>Referrals</u>.

I don't know why I was so surprised. Friend and colleague, George Walther, CSP, CPAE, wrote in his excellent book, <u>Upside Down Marketing</u>:

> "Market researchers have consistently shown that of all the various types of advertising, the most persuasive form is word-of-mouth anecdotes from someone you know. It doesn't matter how many slick commercials and wonderful brochures you see promoting a certain automotive brand, if your neighbor owns one and has complained to you about its poor performance or persistent mechanical problems, you're not likely to buy that type of car."

This information is as good as gold. The easiest sell is when someone else says you are wonderful. The easiest way to get a buyer to pay attention is through third party testimonials: Cialdini's principle of social proof.

Run to your file marked "Nice letters." (Perhaps your file has a more sophisticated name - mine says, Nice Letters! I told you, I don't believe in complicating things!) Look for specifics about your service/product/concept and use these quotes in your sales letters, proposals, follow-ups and brochures. Let your buyer know they have nothing to fear—many others have used your product/ service and have been delighted.

Again, be as specific as you can.

> "The ideas you presented at the program were immediately usable. In fact, after attending your workshop, we exceeded our six-month plan--our profitability zoomed up 23%."
>
> Deborah Ackerman,
> High Achiever Corporation,
> Phoenix, AZ

Now the reader is thinking:

They exceeded their plan by 23%? That High Achiever Corporation has always had a great reputation and they exceeded their plan. I need to find out more about this program.

> "Your software package has saved my sales team hundreds of hours. Before purchasing your software, they turned in expenses late and incomplete. Now, I get them as soon as they get back. Thanks for saving us time, money and aggravation."
>
> Kory Douglas,
> Vice President of Sales,
> Megacolor,
> Ft.Lauderdale, FL

The reader says:

I don't know this Kory person, but if this could make such a difference for him, maybe my team will use it too. I have the exact problem he had—and he seemed to have solved his situation. I'll buy it.

> "You were right. The meeting space was extremely flexible and designed perfectly to encourage education, interaction and networking among my attendees. We will return!"
>
> Michael Brady,
> Executive Director,
> Association of
> the Rich and Famous,
> Scottsdale, AZ

The reader thinks:

Really? Michael thought the meeting space was flexible. I like that Michael—met him at the Association meeting last year. He struck me as being a stickler for details and very perceptive. Hmm! Better look into this property.

Consider beginning your next sales letter/proposal with one, two or three very strong, very specific quotes.

Non–specific spells zero effectiveness

Notice the difference between the quotes you just read and the ones often used:

> You are the greatest thing since sliced bread!
> LH, New York, NY

> Outstanding product!
> ES, Los Angeles, CA

> Great job!
> KM, Dallas, TX

Give me a break! They don't convince anyone of anything. And get a load of those "verifiable names." Very credible! "LH, New York?" Who is that—your momma? "ES" must be your first cousin!

Get permission to quote your delighted client/customer verbatim, and then, read this carefully, use their complete name, title and organization. You'll enhance your credibility and the reliability of the quotations. (Only the anal retentive ones will actually call the people you quoted but everyone will feel better about working with you because they have the social proof they need.)

The quotation becomes your headline

Consider placing your quotation all by itself, at the top of your sales letter. Make it bold. Double space a couple of times and then build on the quote you used.

If, for instance, your quote talks about how your product saves time, your first paragraph should talk more about saving time. If the quote talked about return on investment, your first paragraph should...(Okay, so you get the point!). ⑤

CHAPTER

19

Now That You've Taken Care of Everything Else: Sell, Sell, Sell!

"A genius is a talented person who does his homework."
— Thomas Edison

Y ou have their attention. You've built interest, created desire and need. Your prospect is actually reading your sales letter. (This is a minor miracle! See how well you're doing!)

Finally, you get to the point you've been waiting for. You get to educate your prospect about what you have to offer. Don't get carried away, follow these tips:

<u>Avoid knocking down other ideas, products, solutions</u>.
Let the reader know that every deal/product/solution will take him/her to a certain level of efficiency or effectiveness. Your product/idea/solution will take them higher, farther, faster, easier. (Sounds like I know what you do, doesn't it!)

<u>Be specific</u>.
(Have you read this before?) It is not good to write:

> Our product far exceeds every other on the market.

It is good to write:

> Here are the nine thousand reasons our product has been rated number one in on-time delivery by over 10,000 users.

Tell the truth!

If a flaw exists in your plan (like that you'll come in over budget, past the deadline, etc.), tell them. But build value into it. Answer the questions that are in their minds.

Warren Avis didn't have to tell the world he had a smaller fleet of cars than Hertz, but he knew it could be a potential problem. Instead of hiding behind his facts, he built his advertising theme on them: "We're number two, but we try harder."

Volkswagen did the same when they brought "The Bug" into America in the late 1950s. They knew that American's craved big, beautiful cars; cars that would drive "like a boat." Their little bug would be seen as anything but beautiful. Again, instead of pretending the "flaw" didn't exist, they built on it; For two years, every advertisement started with, "We're ugly but..." and then they went on to talk about fuel efficiency, etc. The rest is history.

Kentucky Fried Chicken nearly went out of business because their chicken was too greasy. Instead of pretending the grease factor didn't exist, they announced their "flaw" and built on it: "Finger-licking good."

Use a headline that states their question:

Isn't it possible that this could cause a delay? Then answer the question truthfully: Yes, it is possible that this may cause a delay in the delivery of the final product. Here are the 14 back ups we have in place to prevent this from occurring. If, even with our 14 back ups, this delay occurs, here is how we are prepared to get you partial shipment before your meeting in Nice.

If your product can't do something, tell them:

> Though we cannot guarantee the sun will shine, we can guarantee an average of 297 days of sunshine and plenty to do even if the weather is less than perfect.

Most sales letter writers believe that if they don't bring up the sensitive issue, it won't come up. (If it doesn't, you'll probably lose the sale!) Bring it up before they do and you build long term relationships based on trust and credibility.

Telling the truth is always the right answer. And the extra benefit to you is more money in the bank. ⑤

CHAPTER

20

HOW TO GET RESULTS WHEN YOU ASK FOR ACTION

"Man who waits with open mouth waits long time for roast goose to fly in."

— Chinese proverb

Oh my goodness.
If there is one thing that writers ***don't*** do, that makes me crazy, this is it.

Often, way too often, I read five–page customized proposals that end with:

- If I can be of further assistance, please do not hesitate to call on me.

- I hope I've answered your questions.

- I look forward to talking to you about the possibility of signing you up for our complete membership package.

P–l–e–e–e–e–a–s–e! When you want action, ask for it!

Here's the deal: Compare those very weak closings with these revisions. Which ones do you think make a more powerful impression? Which closings SELL? Which closings allow you, the salesperson, to take control of the sale?

> • If I can be of further assistance, please do not hesitate to call on me.
>
> OR:
>
> • Phil, I'll phone you June 2 to see what you would like the next step to be.

> • I hope I've answered your questions.
>
> OR:
>
> • Paula, I'll follow-up with you April 21 to answer any additional questions you may have about how we can make this your best meeting ever.

> • I look forward to talking to you about the possibility of signing you up for our complete membership package.
>
> OR:
>
> • Paul, this VIP membership is being offered to you at this price for a limited time. I've enclosed a membership application and high-

> lighted the areas for you to complete. As soon
> as I receive it from you (fax or mail, please), I'll
> phone you to find out a convenient time for
> you to schedule your free health evaluation.
>
> Complete the simple application right now.
> Your health is your most important asset!

"Please review" is not an action statement

Years ago, an employee of a power and gas company attended a public seminar I conducted. When I got to this point in the program, he started laughing. He said it had just dawned on him, why he hadn't received any response from his management regarding the last memo he had sent. He told the group that it was his usual pattern to just go ahead and do whatever he wanted to do, and if necessary, apologize. The last time he did that he had been badly burned.

As a field engineer, working on a project in the field, he had a minor recommendation to change the way the project was going. Because he had so recently been burned, he knew he couldn't just go ahead and do it. He said he wrote the most detailed memo; it was outrageously detailed. He ended it with, "Please review." And he never heard back! It just dawned on him why!

Please review and what? Laugh? Authorize? File? Please review and what? When you want the reader (buyer) to take action, ask!

Show me an action statement

How about this next sentence? Is this an action statement?

Your help is needed to explain a point to the staff.

Nope! No action requested at all. The only action is in the keyboard of the writer! What is the reader (buyer) supposed to do, read your mind? Is she supposed to figure out that what you really meant to say was:

```
Your expertise in this area
would help us to understand
what we're supposed to do with
this project. Our staff meet-
ings are held every Tuesday
at 8:00 a.m. I know how hec-
tic your schedule is though,
so I'll follow-up with your
assistant, Sarah, to see if
this Tuesday or next Tuesday
would be easier for you. I am
really looking forward to your
help.
```

Do you need to tell her all that? Only if will help you get the result you're after! Here is a more concise version:

```
Your recommendations (advice,
help, suggestions, expertise)
on the ABC project would help
us complete this project on
time. Would this Tuesday's
staff meeting, or next Tues-
day, fit better into your
```

> schedule to meet with us? I'll
> call you Monday to see which
> day is easier for you.

Now you're asking for action!

So here it is: A proven way to write a sales letter that will get you results:

1. Get your reader's attention by telling him specifically what is in it for him.

2. Tell the reader why she needs to be interested in what you have to say.

3. Prove it's the truth.

4. Describe the benefits of your idea/product/service.

5. Explain the next step clearly. 💲

PART IV

TIPS THAT WILL INCREASE YOUR READABILITY

I'm trying to sell something–how important is readability?

You have a minimum of five seconds to grab your reader's attention. The easier you make it on that reader to understand, believe and see, the better your chances of nailing the sale.

Don't skim over this section; it'll improve your writing skills dramatically.

WRITE TO INCREASE YOUR SELLING POWER

"In composing, as a general rule, run a pen through every other word you have written; you have no idea what vigor it will give your style."

— Sidney Smith

"It is well to remember that grammar is common speech formulated. Usage is only a test. I would prefer a phrase that was easy and unaffected to a phrase that was grammatical."

— W. Somerset Maugham

"A writer who finds everything interesting makes almost everything boring."

— Jack Miles, editor,
Los Angeles Time Book Review as quoted by Allan Cox

Obstacles like incorrect grammar, wrong punctuation, poor word usage and typos direct your reader's attention from your message. They lessen the impact of your words.

Here are some tips to help smooth the road:

- <u>Write in present tense</u>

    "I suggest" instead of: "I would like to suggest," "It is his suggestion," "He suggested."

- <u>Keep focused on the buyer</u>

    "You, you, you!" Use twice as many "you, your" words as you do "I, me" words.

- <u>Use headlines</u>

    Show them how they'll benefit from your service/ product. Use a headline for each benefit.

- <u>Use subheads</u>

    These are short statements in between the headlines detailing each benefit. (Check out how I've used them to help you read this book.)

- <u>Keep it short</u>

    Your readers are as limited on time as you are— make it easy for them. Use short, simple words. Short sentences. Short paragraphs.

How the readers move their eyes over a page

A large American research company conducted eyeball studies to determine how people actually read. By watching the patterns of the eyes, they discovered that 64% of the American population reads only three–quarters of the way across a page!

We read in a "Z" pattern. Picture the "Z." Take your eyes about three–quarters of the way across the first line and then skim the middle, look for the white space that indicates the end of the paragraph. That's how 64% read.

- For maximum readability, sentences should average 14 to 18 words and paragraphs should average five sentences each.

Check word readability and copy length

Rudolph Flesch has published a mathematical formula for figuring out the readability level of your writing. (His exercise is great if you like math and want to do it the old fashioned way! You may want to simply click on your Grammar checker on your Mac or PC! Most software programs have a word counter on their programs. You can easily see how long your sentences and paragraphs are. Many programs will do the math for you and even suggest alternate ways of phrasing your ideas to ensure that you keep it readable. Check it out!)

- **Be specific.**

Tell me you've worked in 112 different counties, not "many" international venues.

- **Use long copy when it is clearly focused on the reader and you have fascinating stuff to tell them**
- **Use understatement before overstatement**

Don't try to appear better than you really are. Promise big but be sure to deliver bigger.

- **Avoid cliches (like the plague)**

Sorry! Couldn't help it! Not only are cliches outdated and trite, not only are they boring to read, in today's global marketplace, they are inappropriate. Consider how the person, using English as a second language, will feel and react to a statement such as: *We'll finalize these arrangements as soon as we run it up the flagpole to ensure there are no red flags we've missed.*

Additionally, many cliches are sport oriented and many non–athletes may not understand what you mean. (Talk to me about meeting around the *kitchen table* instead of the *war room*, and I can envision much more being accomplished. Doesn't feel comfortable? Why not? Point made.)

- **Be absolutely certain you are constantly writing about how your buyer can save, gain, or accomplish because of your product/service**

  If you can't write about what they'll save, gain or accomplish, tell them how they'll avoid risk, worry, loss, mistakes, or embarrassment.

- **Write as if you're writing to one person**

  Write to the person you expect to act on your message.

- **Read your letter out loud so you can hear it flow—or not**

  Hearing the words gives it a different perspective and it will help you find those pesky communications problems.

- **The only way to hold your reader's (buyer's) attention is to write about what you/your product/your service can do for the customer/client**

  Do not concentrate (at first) on what the product is, focus on what it does.

- **When you have a lot of information—but it doesn't really connect**

  Simply "bullet" each item or piece of information. Make a

list as I have done here. For example, you want to tell me about all the facilities at your property:

- A complete health club conveniently located.

- The largest meeting room space available in the downtown area

- Door-to-door shuttle available 24 hours

Always, always remember:

√ why you're writing

√ what you want to say

√ what you want to accomplish

√ what exact action or reaction you want from your reader. $

CHAPTER 22

THESE EXPRESSIONS WILL KILL YA'!

"A powerful agent is the right word. Whenever we come upon one of those intensely right words...the resulting effect is physical as well as spiritual."

— Mark Twain

What would a book on writing be if it didn't have a list of *stupid writing tricks*—outdated, overused words and cliches? Here is mine—with commentary (What did you expect? No comments?!)

Thanking you in advance
Variation:
Thanking you in advance for your anticipated cooperation.

It doesn't matter to me if you own the publishing company publishing this book or if you're the most junior sales person on the team: Who are you to think you can thank someone before they have done anything?

Thank them when you mean it—not before the fact.

Think back to a time when you received a thank you for a job well done. Have it in your mind? Good. Were you thinking of a time when someone tacked on to his or her request:

> *Thanking you in advance for your anticipated cooperation in this matter.*

Or, are you thinking about a separate note of thanks?

Yeah, I know, of course, it's a separate note. "Thanking you in advance" doesn't mean thank you. It means, "Do it, sucker!"

Thank them when you mean it. Thank them after the fact and in a separate note.

Please feel free to call

In the U.S. of A., no one gets a "free feel!" This is a meaningless expression that has even less meaning (is that possible?) when used internationally. Delete.

Prioritize, finalize

Just because you place an ending on a word, doesn't mean you can create a new word! We do this most commonly with the endings, "-ize" and "-ate."

Final*ize*,   American*ize*,
schedul*ize*,   agend*ize*,
Canadian*ize*,   summar*ize*,

and
administr*ate*,
orient*ate*,
filtr*ate*.

Don't! Use real words in your writing because what you write will stick around and haunt you forever!

I had this boss, when I worked In Queens, NY, who would "combinize." Yes, you read that right!! Every time he would write *combinize*, I would change it back to *combine*. Every time I would write combine, he would upgrade it to combinize! This went on for five months! Finally, I couldn't stand it anymore. I went into his office, with two dictionaries, and in my sweetest possible voice said, "Phil, I can't seem to locate combinize in these dictionaries." He took the books, checked them out, handed them back and said, "You know, you're right. It isn't there. But it should be." We continued to combinize!!!

As per your request

Back in 1938 (yep, you read that right, too!), New York Life Insurance decided to train their people in better writing. There hadn't been any research into what made good writing, however, so they commissioned a group of researchers to develop writing guidelines. In 1942, they came out with their list of recommendations.

Every five to six years since then, this research is revalidated. One of the recommendations of that 1942 study – and is still valid today – is that writers not use Latin in their writing; instead, when they are writing to people who speak English, they should use English!

What does "as per your request" mean? Consider these alternatives:

√ As you requested...

√ Here is the information we discussed...

When you're writing to people who speak Latin, go for it. Otherwise keep it to standard English!

Just to remind you

Consider these common phrases:

- Just to thank you...

- Just a note...

- Just a memo regarding...

What does the word "Just" mean in each of those examples? *Only ...nothing much...insignificant!* Hey, they pay little enough attention to your documents in the first place! Why would you belittle the content of the message or the value of your time?

Drop the word *just* and get on with it!

To my knowledge
As far as I know

These phrases belittle the writer's time and the message's content. What do they mean? How far do you know? How much knowledge do you have? Replace those demeaning statements with:

- *Based on....*

- *Based on* my discussion with Crystal, Kim and Kyle, here are the department's figures. (You know you should have discussed it with everyone in the department, but don't tell them what you didn't do, tell them what you did do.)

Obviously

Okay folks, think about this. If something is obvious, WHY would you need to write it? (To make someone feel really bad!!!)

Years ago, I used to recommend *evidently, apparently,* or *clearly* as good replacements. O–o–o–ps! My mistake! I was reading an article by William Safire in <u>The New York Times</u>. His contention is that most words—not all—but most words that end in -ly are not only needless, but are insulting. As his examples, he used *evidently, apparently* and *clearly*!!

If something is evident, what does that mean? *It means it is! It's clear! We all know it.* So why are we writing it, if not to stick someone's face in it! (Never a good reason to write!)

Before you use a word that ends in -ly, ask yourself, *Will this help my reader?* Ten per cent of the time it will make a positive transition; 90% of the time it's needless or insulting.

In order to

Were you ever taught that you couldn't begin a sentence with a preposition? Yes, you can!! What does the Bible begin with? That's right! A preposition! Of course, you can begin a sentence with a preposition. (No one has revised the Bible yet!)

You can *end* a sentence with a preposition, too! There is a story about two undergraduates and the first one said:

"Where do you go to school at?"

The other one, with his nose in the air, said,

> "It doesn't really matter where I go to school, but where *I* go to school, we have learned, never, ever to end a sentence with a preposition."

> "Oh, I'm sorry," said the first undergrad. "Where do you go to school at, dirtbag?!"

Winston Churchill ended many of his sentences in his autobiography with prepositions. When his young editor reviewed the manuscript, he couldn't believe Churchill would end his sentences that way. He revised each sentence so it would no longer end in a preposition. When Churchill got the manuscript back, he was furious. He wrote his editor a very caustic note, started it off with a few swear words and then wrote:

> "Put these (the prepositions) back where I had them to begin with. This is an imposition up with which I will not put."

When the preposition is the least awkward of all possible choices, you can both begin and end a sentence with it.

Needless to say

If it's needless to say, don't say it!

More than happy to

How can you be *more than happy to?* That would have to be orgasmic and that is not what this book is about! (It's like being "more than welcome." How can you be *more than welcome?* You're either welcome or you're not!)

> Use the word that describes the emotion:
> happy...pleased...glad...delighted. (*More than happy* is foolish!)

Yes. There are more cliches—lots more. If you get rid of the ones listed here, you'll be writing more powerfully. Look for all the stupid stuff other people put in their letters/ proposals/ brochures and you'll know what to leave out of yours! ⑤

CHAPTER

23

IF YOU WANT THEM TO READ IT—MAKE IT READABLE!

"Half the world is composed of people who have some-thing to say and can't, and the other half who have nothing to say and keep on saying it."

— Robert Frost

Even before the information superhighway, we were stuck in traffic! Between meetings at corporate, sales meeting with clients/customers, industry association meetings, trade shows, and telephone tag, writing proposals, sales letters and follow-up letters, and a little thing called life (read: family, home, dog, gym), we had no time. Add in the immediacy of everything we do today (Can you believe they can now page us even on an airplane?), and it's easy to see how we are on overload.

What is the first thing to go (besides life?)? Reading! We don't read stuff. We look at it (unless of course, it's about holiday, pay or vacation scheduling or someone at work who we really like or someone we've been waiting to see get the shaft! Then we read!).

We, and they, our all-important buyer, need to simplify our

lives. We need to get home at a reasonable hour. So we take information highway shortcuts and off ramps (is this getting to be a bit much?!), and simply and quickly we skim our messages. Not only do we often miss important stuff but they, our all-important buyers, miss important stuff—our important stuff— and they don't even know it!

How can you make it easier for them to read your sales proposal?

You can make the letter or proposal pleasing to the eye. We're not talking artistic, we're talking readability. Use the elements I've listed below and you'll see for yourself how it will enhance your letters:

- **Lots of white space**

  Gives them the impression that your message won't be too much of a bother to read, won't take up too much of their time...might as well read it.

- **Lists**

  Most of us love reading *down* the page/screen...gets us closer to the end. We hate being forced to read across the page and, as I mentioned earlier, 64% of us don't or won't.

  (One client made the window on his computer screen smaller so he only displays about three-quarters of the message. He skims it to decide if it's something that is interesting enough to motivate him to open the full box. Scary, isn't it!)

- **Short sentences**

  For maximum readability, keep your sentences averaging 14 to 18 words.

- **Short paragraphs**

  Paragraphs should average five sentences. One sentence paragraphs are fine, by the way.

- **Highlight: Use bold, *italics*, <u>underline</u>,**

  Put boxes around important points.

- **Don't overdo these elements**

  Too much bold, italic, boxes, etc, will take you forever and they'll get nuts! Less is more. (Always wondered how I could use that expression... I mean I know so many things in life that it doesn't apply to!) ☻

EPILOGUE

WHY BOTHER WRITING WELL?

"Wealth is the product of man's capacity to think."
— Ayn Rand

"The difference between the right word and the almost right word is the difference between lightning and the lightning bug."
— Mark Twain

So there you have it. Almost. Every idea you'll ever need to write more professionally, more productively, more powerfully... every idea you'll need to use writing as a tool to get you the results you want...the sales...the profits...the prestige. The question for you is, Are you going to use the ideas? Why should you? What's in it for you?

Here's a quickie. Answer the question:

> Why should I bother to implement these
> new writing strategies?

Here's my list:

Clear, powerful, persuasive writing will:

- Get you the result you want (money, money, money!!!)
- Increase your esteem and professionalism in the eyes of others (maybe your own, too!)
- Enhance your image, reputation and credibility
- Save you time and energy
- Eliminate embarrassment, confusion, expensive redos
- Cover your assets and be likely to keep you out of court
- Help you to be more responsive to your customer
- Position you to beat out the competition

So now it's up to you.

The Hardest Part

In the almost 2,000 workshops I've presented on Power Writing—I always find this the hardest part. I know that the strategies you've just read about can dramatically change your life. I know that with practice, you can not only save yourself substantial amounts of time, you can easily stop the destructive procrastinating behavior that most sales professionals exhibit when it comes to writing.

In fact, I know that the practical and specific techniques in this book will teach you to actually use your written documents as a powerful new sales tool to beat out your competition and make more money.

But what have you learned? And what will you do with it? If you're really interested in changing the way you write, take the time (right now, please) to list 25 techniques you've learned. List the strategies that will help you to be a more professional, persuasive and profitable writer. (Yes. You may look back! Consider this an open book test!)

1.
2.
3.
4.
5.
6.
7.
8.
9.
10.
11.
12.
13.
14.
15.
16.
17.
18.
19.
20.
21.
22.

23.

24.

25.

Congratulations! Now, just one more thing... (Why did I just feel like Colombo?!)

Look over your list and find the two ideas that really hit home for you—the two ideas that you know will definitely make a difference to you when you implement them. Write them here:

1._____

2._____

Start with those two. Write them on a sticky note and stick them on your desk, or have them pop up on your computer a few times each day. During the first month, only deal with using and perfecting those two strategies *you identified as techniques that will absolutely help you.* Once you have those as new habits (it'll take about three weeks to unlearn the old habit and three more weeks to learn the new one), find two more...then two more...then two more.... You'll be amazed.

> *"The value of an idea lies in the using of it."*
>
> — Thomas Edison

> *"Our grand business is not to see what lies dimly in the distance, but to do what lies clearly at hand."*
>
> — Thomas Carlyle

Happy Selling!